CHIMPS

Sandie Lee Books

Chimpanzee

The chimpanzee is not a monkey, it is an ape - monkey's have tails and the chimp does not. This animal is in the Hominidae family, along with orangutans, gorillas and humans. The chimpanzee species has been around between 4 to 6 million years. This animal is very intelligent and can even learn some aspects of the human language. Let's dive deeper into the fascinating world of the chimpanzee. We will discover what it eats, how it uses tools and so much more.

Where in the World?

Did you know the chimpanzee only lives in a small part of Africa? Due to deforestation of the chimp's natural habitat, it can only be found in western Africa. This includes from the congo to Uganda, Rwanda, Burundi and Tanzania. This animal likes the tropical rain forests, woodlands, swamp forests and the grasslands.

The Body of a Chimpanzee

Did you know the chimp can be very large? A male chimpanzee can grow to be around 5.6 feet tall and weigh around 150 pounds, females will be smaller. The arms of a chimp are 1.5 times longer than its body and definitely longer than its legs. The chimp is also covered in thick black fur.

The Skin of a Chimpanzee

Did you know like you and I, the chimpanzee has skin? Not all parts of this animal has fur. Its face, fingers, palms of the hands and soles of its feet do not have any hair on them. The color of this skin can range from pink to very dark. The skin will darken as the chimp ages.

What a Chimpanzee Eats

Did you know chimps are omnivorous? Even though some books portray chimpanzee's eating nothing but bananas, they do eat a lot of other things. Chimpanzees like various fruits, nuts, leaves, seeds, mushrooms and flowers. This animal also likes to eat meat occasionally. It will hunt insects and even small monkeys.

The Chimpanzee's Special

Did you know the chimpanzee can use "tools"? This animal will strip a stick of its leaves to poke into a termite mound or a beehive. The chimp has also learned to use rocks as hammers to crack open nuts. Larger rocks are dropped on tougher foods to break them open, as well.

Chimpanzees and Grooming

Did you know this great ape will groom itself and others? The chimpanzee uses grooming in a social manner. A chimp will groom another to pick out dirt, parasites and dead skin. A chimp will also tend to another's cuts or scrapes. Sometimes, this animal uses grooming to make friends and to comfort one another.

The Chimpanzee's Defense

Did you know the chimp is a powerful fighter? Chimps may engage in a bloody battle over food, mates and territory. They will bite their victims with their sharp canine teeth (front fangs). They will also hit, stomp, kick and pull the other chimp's fur. Sometimes, they will also drag their victim around on the ground.

The Chimpanzee as Prey

Did you know even though the chimp is a large animal, it is still hunted? Chimps are hunted by the leopard. This cat will not usually hunt a healthy adult chimp, but will hunt the young or very old. Man also hunts the chimp for its meat. This is called "bushmeat"

Chimp Talk

Did you know chimpanzees have different ways of communicating? This animal uses a sound called a, "pant-hoot." This is done in greeting or when calling to other chimps that are far away. The chimp will also grunt, scream when it is upset or even laugh when it is playing or being tickled.

The Chimpanzee Mom

Did you know the female chimp carries her baby for 9 months? The female's rump will turn a bright pink when she is ready to mate. She can have her first baby at around 14 years-old. Mom chimp will care for her baby until it is around 5 years-old. However, the baby still stays within the family unit when it is older.

The Baby Chimp

Did you know the baby chimp is totally dependant on its mom? A newborn chimp only weighs about 4 pounds when it is born. The baby will nurse milk from its mother for about 5 years. When the baby chimp is born it has a white tuft of fur on its rump. The baby clings to its mother's belly for safety and warmth.

Chimps at Rest

Did you know the chimp can spend 6 to 8 hours foraging for food? When this animal is not looking for and eating food, it is resting. Adult chimps rest high among the trees or sitting on the ground in a group. They may not always sleep when at rest, sometimes they will engage in social grooming.

Chimps at Play

Did you know baby chimps will tumble and play with each other? Baby chimps will wrestle and chase each other around. They also watch the adults and will mimic their behaviour when they play. Adult chimps may tickle their little ones and will also swing from tree to tree. Happy chimps will embrace and even kiss each other.

Life of a Chimpanzee

Did you know the chimp can live to be around 50 years-old in the wild? Chimps spend their lives in a community. This group can consist of up to 60 individual animals. Sometimes the chimp will travel a short distance with 5 other members of its group. Chimps spend a lot of time in the trees where it is safe.

Quiz

Question 1: What is the difference between a monkey and a chimp?

Answer 1: Monkey's have tails. Chimps do not

Question 2: What color is the chimps thick fur?

Answer 2: Black

Question 3: Like human's, what do chimps use in their daily life?

Answer 3: Tools (rocks and sticks)

Question 4: What might an angry chimp do?

Answer 4: Stomp, hit, kick and pull another chimps fur

Question 5: How long does mom carry her baby chimp for?

Answer 5: 9 months

Thank you for checking out another addition from Sandie Lee Books! Make sure to check out Amazon.com for many other great titles.